Sleep

Written by Jill Eggleton
Illustrated by Philip Webb

The tiger is asleep.

The bird
dropped a feather.

The tiger is asleep.

The bird
dropped a leaf.

The tiger is asleep.

The bird
dropped a seed.

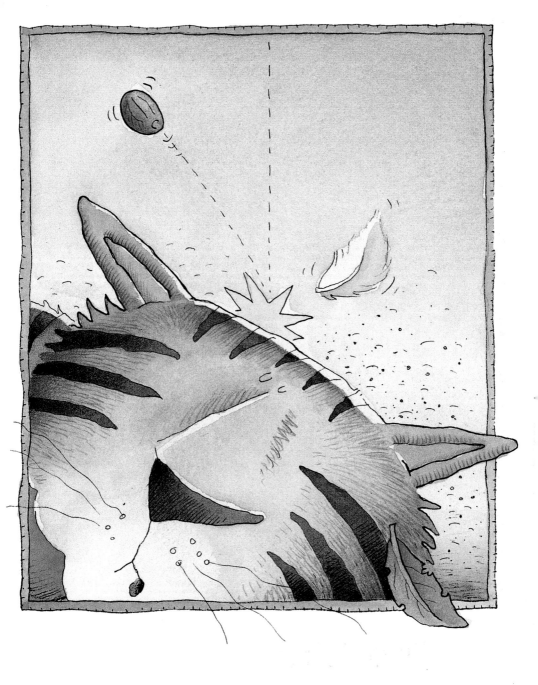

The tiger is asleep.

The monkey
dropped a banana.

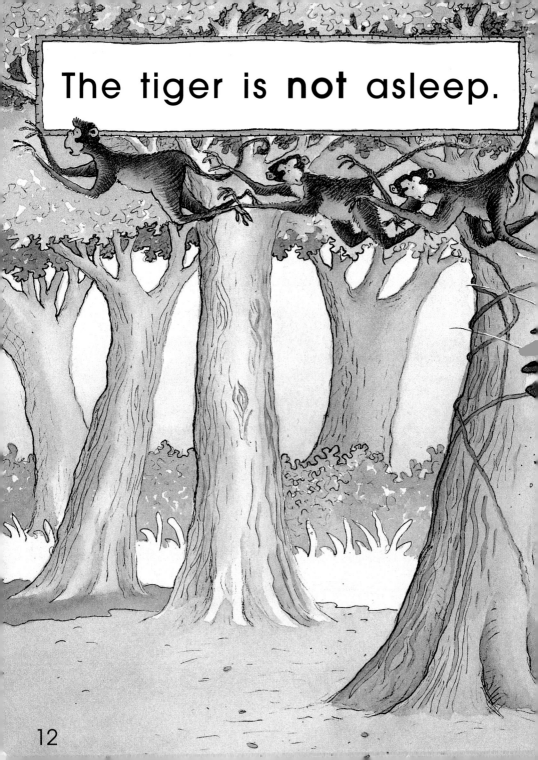

The tiger is **not** asleep.

13

A Story Map

▬▬▬ Guide Notes

Title: Sleepy Tiger
Stage: Emergent – Magenta

Genre: Fiction
Approach: Guided Reading
Processes: Thinking Critically, Exploring Language, Processing Information
Written and Visual Focus: Story Map
Word Count: 41

FORMING THE FOUNDATION

Tell the children that the story is about a tiger asleep in the jungle and a bird trying to wake the tiger.
Talk to them about what is on the front cover. Read the title and the author / illustrator.
'Walk' through the book focussing on the illustrations and talking to the children about what is happening on each page. Talk about the monkey and its part in the story.
Leave pages 12-13 for prediction.

Read the text together.

THINKING CRITICALLY
(sample questions)

After the reading
- Why do you think the bird wants to wake the tiger?
- What do you think the tiger might do now it is awake?

EXPLORING LANGUAGE
(ideas for selection)

Terminology
Title, cover, author, illustrator, illustrations

Vocabulary
Interest words: tiger, asleep, bird, dropped, feather, leaf, seed, monkey, banana
High-frequency words: the, is, a